To Find the Gold

To
Find the
GOLD

Poems by

SUSAN LUDVIGSON

1990

LOUISIANA STATE UNIVERSITY PRESS

Baton Rouge and London

Copyright © 1986, 1987, 1988, 1989, 1990 by Susan Ludvigson
All rights reserved
Manufactured in the United States of America

First printing
99 98 97 96 95 94 93 92 91 90   5 4 3 2 1
Designer: Amanda McDonald Key
Typeface: Goudy Old Style
Typesetter: G&S Typesetters, Inc.
Printer and binder: Thomson-Shore, Inc.

The author gratefully acknowledges the editors of the following periodicals, in which many of the poems herein first appeared: *Defining the Holy: A Chapbook, Memphis State Review, Nation, Paris Atlantic, Quarterly West, River Styx, Southern Poetry Review, Tar River Poetry, Southern Review, Pacific Review.* "To Enter" and "Paris Aubade" were first published in *Georgia Review.* "Laura" was first published in *America.*

The author would like to thank the Witter Bynner Foundation and the North Carolina Arts Council for fellowships that helped support her during the writing of this book. Thanks also to Winthrop College for arranging a flexible teaching schedule. She also thanks Stephen Corey, Harriet Doar, Scott Ely, Judy Goldman, Dannye Romine, and Julie Suk for their valuable suggestions about poems in this book.

Library of Congress Cataloging-in-Publication Data

Ludvigson, Susan
    To find the gold : poems / by Susan Ludvigson.
        p.   cm.
    ISBN 0-8071-1599-1 (alk. paper). — ISBN 0-8071-1600-9
    (pbk. : alk. paper)
    I. Title.
PS3562.U27T6   1990
811'.54—dc20   89-28159
                                                      CIP

For Scott

CONTENTS

Part Three

Part One

THE GOLD SHE FINDS:
ON THE LIFE OF CAMILLE CLAUDEL, SCULPTOR

Sculpture is born of the need to touch, from the almost maternal joy of holding clay between one's hands. —Camille Claudel

I showed her where to find the gold, but the gold she finds is truly hers. —Auguste Rodin

Mlle. Claudel's sculpture is very different from Rodin's. She picks and gathers the light like a bouquet, unlike Rodin, who presents a compact block that shoves it back. —Philippe Berthelot

Camille Claudel is the most considerable woman artist at the present hour. —Camille Mauclair, 1895

Along with Berthe Morisot, Camille Claudel is the authentic representative of the female genius. —Gustave Kahn, 1905

In Paris, Camille mad . . . huge and looking filthy, speaking incessantly in a monotonous and metallic voice . . . one had to intervene . . . and there it is for thirty years. —Paul Claudel, 1909, 1911

I.

THE LITTLE CHATELAINE, 1870

A pitcher shatters, red wine spilled
to the tiled kitchen floor
and spreading. It's a map, the child
thinks absently, tucking her feet
behind the chair rung. The usual
voices raised to the usual pitch
fly past her, a swarm of blackbirds.
Camille feels her mother's rage,
but it is like wind that can only leak in
around windows and doors, through
small cracks. Nothing to fear
when her face contracts,
or from her father's bellowing.
The child gives a sign
to her brother, excuses herself
and slips away. Animals rearrange
their bodies in the evening clouds,
where the faces of saints
are known to appear.
She spends half an hour, hoping
for Our Lady of Fatima,
who keeps herself busy, embroidering.
By bedtime, the moon is a cousin
who died last year. His face tells Camille
he suffered—the pockmarks still there,
his brow crinkled. André, she calls
through the trees, and hearing
no answer, answers her mother.

II.

SISTER AND BROTHER IN THE FOREST OF VILLENEUVE, 1879

They climb to the few flat stretches
of massive stone that jut, savage monuments,
to the sky. Clothes thrown aside,
they sit, she clutching her knees,
he leaning back on an elbow, a book open
next to him. He reads to her—
Alfred de Vigny. His own poems show a mass
of chestnut hair to her hips, and blue eyes
he describes as a color encountered
only in novels. As Paul's light skin
grows pink in the sun, she sketches him,
page after page of young Roman,
that sweet torso lithe as birch.

Thunderclouds move in with the stealth
of their mother. When the rain comes,
lashing them in a sudden wind, they struggle
into wet clothes gleefully, slide down,
then dash to their small cave, with its cache
of candles. In hazy light, her joke drawings,
made to look prehistoric, take on
a luminous glow. A small horse
leaps across one wall, a dart in its flank.

III.

THE MEETING, 1884

My dear Paul,

Today I met the master, Rodin!
Do you remember my meeting
at the École des Beaux-Arts?
How after M. Dubois saw my bust
of you, the one when you're
thirteen, he asked if I were
Rodin's student? That Rodin.
When he took me into his studio
where he's in the midst of an epic,
The Gates of Hell—incredible work!—
I trembled. Paul, some of the figures
looked like mine—especially
the women's features, but there's a weight,
an authority, that's not me.
And M. Rodin himself—well. He's got eyes
like diamonds, that look as if he's trying
to drill to the bottom of everyone,
and a great shaggy head, with a nose
imperious as yours, but bigger!
When he talks his nostrils flare.
He has the air of a nervous horse, always
in motion, starting at noises,
and skinny legs that almost prance.
He took one long look at *Old Helen*
and my *Bust of a Woman with Closed Eyes,*
and announced that I'd be his assistant.
This alone, little Paul, was worth
the move to Paris. I'll be helper,
student, apprentice, and do my own work.
It's as if I'd lived the rest of my life
in the forest, not knowing that all paths out
would join in one distant spot—right here.

IV.

NOTE TO RODIN AFTER *SEA FOAM*, 1884

Nothing prepared me for this.
Not even those first giddy weeks
when we talked of taking a steamer
to Africa, leaving everyone behind.
Before I met you I thought I knew
the human form, but what I know now
is deeper than skin and muscle,
deeper than bone. You discovered
something quiet in me, and made it grow,
just as you lift a breast in your hands,
gently blowing, breathing
more life into it. I am no longer
that country girl with talent,
but a woman whose joy has found
its voice in marble.

v.

THE ETERNAL IDOL, 1887

My dear Paul,

Imagine my surprise this morning,
walking into the studio, to find
M. Rodin sitting before two models
posed like lovers, the woman
on her knees on a low table,
leaning back and holding her toes
with her hands, perfectly balanced,
the man kneeling before her, pressed
into her, his head between her breasts,
his mouth more caress than kiss on her
white skin. All the while,
M. Rodin was sketching, frenzied,
throwing one piece of paper
after the next to the floor. My *Cacountala,*
in clay, stood in the corner, like
a mirror to these lovers, who, if they
shifted position slightly, could see
themselves in elemental form. It was
as if my figures had been touched by a god
and brought to life. Everything was silent
except for the sound of ripped paper
and Rodin's breathing—always louder
than anyone's! The models, though,
for the first five minutes I stood there,
didn't seem to breathe at all.
It was like a dream

broken by a bird hitting the window.
The couple unfolded themselves, and Rodin
and I went for a coffee. Paul, he had
tears in his eyes, and told me—oh
many things. Rose, he says,
is getting arthritic, her knees creak
when she walks, and sometimes it's painful
even to get up out of her chair.
Poor Rose. It would be awful to be old.
But worse for him, who feels he lives
inside his own Gates of Hell (no wonder

that work has all the pathos of his genius!)—
one or another of the children always sick,
and that woman. Paul, I feel his spirit
in me, and when my hands are filled with clay,
I have the texture of flesh in my fingers
long before the casting, I know the tension
in each tendon, the way eyes hold
their memories intact, how sorrow
animates a body, even in rapture.

VI.
THE TOWER OF THE CHATEAU D'ISLETTE
IN TOURAINE, 1887

In this vast cylinder
we are dancers floating
up a spiral staircase
to the room where dozens
of arrow slits let in
the moon's damp light,
making a crown of leaves
across your forehead.
I love my whole body
wet, exhausted.
Each foggy dawn
I lie in half sleep.
Always those fingers open
my thighs, your big hands
warm as the rising sun,
while swallows circle outside.
At noon we stand on the bridge
tossing chunks of bread
to the lazy trout.
I like to complain
of my muscles aching.
You grin.
You put a piece of brioche
on my tongue and say,
Here is my flesh.
All afternoon and evening
wind churns the light until,
red as burgundy, it follows
us back to bed.

VII.
"LE CLOS PAYEN," 1888

Her art has the inner light, is perforated, cut out like stained glass, it
welcomes and captures the light. It is in this way that her art resembles the
art of jade.

—Philippe Berthelot

My dear Paul,

The house M. Rodin rented for us
is falling to ruins, but it has charms.
I've been sweeping
cobwebs from the salon we'll use
for work, which at first looked
like our old cave—the light
through those dirty windows so dim
we found a bat contentedly sleeping,
dangling from the chandelier.
Paul, he had the bedroom
redone as a surprise for me—but frankly,
just between us, it has the look
of a bordello, great heavy drapes
of velvet (red!) trimmed in gold.
There's a Louis XIV dressing table
I do like, and a scrolled
hand mirror with distorted glass
that makes me look a bit fat,
though it's gorgeous. I think he found it
at the flea market. Most important,
we can get away from Rose,
who's begun to hound him.

I make him cassoulet and roasted lamb,
even attempted a tarte the other day—
peach—that wasn't bad.
I plan work on a figure I'll call
Young Woman with a Sheaf. I have
the drawings already, know everything
about her stance, a certain modesty
she'll suggest, but I haven't yet
got the expression. I've also just made

a drawing of you, my dear, in colored
pencil. It's your pouty look,
the one that enchants the girls.
I hardly need you to pose any more,
your face is so clear
it rises to greet me mornings.
Lately I don't remember my dreams,
though some days I wake with a sense
of colors swirling around me, great
sweeps of it. Maybe that girl
with the sheaf has made a broom,
is replacing the debris of this house
with deep blues and purples, like sky
just before sunrise.

VIII.

LETTER TO RODIN FROM THE CHATEAU D'ISLETTE IN TOURAINE, WHERE CAMILLE WENT ALONE, PERHAPS PREGNANT, 1889

Seigneur,

I'm writing you again because
I have nothing else to do. And to tell you
it's wonderful here—the hay's just
been cut, and the wheat and oats,
and the meadow smells of lavender.
Madame C. tells me that if we like
we can take all our meals
in the small conservatory that looks
both ways to the garden.
I had lunch there today, and it's
lovely—every color imaginable
of that flower I'd rather not name,
and dahlias, giant and dwarf,
and hollyhocks and yellow lilies.
She tells me I can bathe in the river.
Her daughter and the maid do,
and it's perfectly safe.
Would you mind? It would save me
trips to the baths in Azay
and I could use that time to sketch.

Love, I sleep naked to let myself pretend
you're here, but the mornings
are so disappointing. Please hurry!
Would you buy me a dark blue
bathing suit, please—if you can
find it—with white piping. Try
the Bon Marché.

Above all, no more deception.
Keep your promise and we'll be
in paradise.

IX.
"LA DEMOISELLE ÉLUE," 1890

Ah! I really loved her and with all the more sad ardor by the evident signs I felt that never would she take certain steps to engage her whole spirit and that she was keeping herself inviolable against queries to her heart's solidity.
—Claude Debussy, in a letter to Robert Godet

My dear Paul,

Do you recall the musician I mentioned
I'd met at Robert Godet's? Debussy?
I care nothing for music normally,
as you know, but how I wish you could hear
him play. It takes me back to Villeneuve.
I can see us whirling across those fields
from the giant rocks, a pair of hummingbirds,
and he gives me the feeling too
of poems you read me that summer
you were twelve, and I was sixteen.
Something about him lets me be a girl
again, Paul. A splendid man!
I fear refusing him
is another grand mistake. Rodin
is jealous. Fine. He has his tarts.
In truth, I'm close to Claude the way
I'm close to you—and he's a refuge
from that world where the pain keeps spreading.
I begin to think our saggy-skinned Rose
is installed forever, no matter
that she shakes her fist at him every day.
Most of the time, I feel my own youth
draining away like an August stream.
Affection ebbs too, yet I can't
make a break. I try to fall in love
with Claude, who's my age, and adores me.
He's adopted my passion for Japanese drawing
and says he'd give up green-eyed Gabrielle.
So why does that pot-bellied old man
keep my soul? He's like a cancer
that creates a gorgeous fever,
all the while gnawing away at the heart
of everything.

X.

LETTER TO RODIN FROM TOURAINE, 1893

What joy to wake from a dream of you
and not desire you! All this time,
my hands busy in plaster, you occupied
my body like a tenant. Wherever
I turned I saw women with your eye,
their flesh blushing under my frank look.
Mornings the windows filled with pollen,
and I laughed, feeling your beautiful
sneeze—the way you throw your whole
head back, like a fine horse neighing.
Today I wonder if you're rowing
on a lake somewhere with a girl
whose auburn hair makes her partly
me. I don't even care. I'm separate
just now, I'm Camille, who drinks
beer alone in a café, the buzz of voices
around her like a waltz,
wanting only earth between her fingers,
earth under her feet.

XI.
NOTES FOR *THE VANISHED GOD,*
OR *THE BESEECHER,* 1894

At last you were "yourself," totally free of Rodin's influence, your
imagination was as great as your craft.
                    —*Letter from Eugene Blot to Camille Claudel, 1932*

I want to feel the weight of her knees
on the stone, and the pain
of kneeling there so long, but she
will have gone beyond the physical,
into a realm where he is all
that can touch her. Eyes and arms will lift
in an agony of prayer,
she'll be pure supplication,
and may be pregnant.
There'll be a sense that she knows
the outcome, does not expect
the god to relent or reappear.
But there is nothing else for her.
She'll ache for him without faith,
without choice, in sheer despair.

XII.

THREE WORKS, 1895–1897

1. *Maturity*, Plaster, 1895

My dear Paul,

I fear it's more and more hopeless.
It's as if he's a tree grown
with branches intertwined
in another, one gnarled and stronger
with age, and he can't disentangle
himself without snapping
too many limbs. Never mind
that my green shoots got mingled
with his.

At last, I've got us in plaster.
Mother Rose with her fist clenched
against me, he with his arm
clasped around her, protecting her.
I'm on my knees as always,
clutching his hand, and he's turned
to her even as his body yearns
in my direction. In bronze,
it will be more mythic, but
for now, we're ourselves, raw.
The harpy wins.

2. *The Little Chatelaine* II, 1895

My dear Paul,

I keep trying to get *The Little Chatelaine*
right, less haunted, but the eyes
stay blind, the face more grieved
than mine in every conception.
Some days I'm not sure which of us
came first. My hair too was braided like that
at seven. I can still feel Mother
yanking it, making me cry, and telling
you and Louise that I was a baby.
You and lovely Louise, who did

17

all the right things—married, produced
proper children. Paul, tell me the truth
when you come next month. Look
into my eyes and see if you see the shadow.
Look at her and tell me who I am.

3. *Clotho*, Marble, 1897

After all, the body knows just as much as the soul, the details of the
anatomy are worth those of psychoanalysis.

—*Paul Claudel*

Toothless, breasts
crumpled paper, she can scarcely
carry the dross of her life,
hair a mass of twisted ropes
that weigh on her head,
so that she must tilt it
to one side, even to stand.

How many times have a man's hands
gripped the old woman's calves?
Pressing loose skin,
does he bruise her ankles?

She sees her path,
even with rheumy eyes,
and keeps her direction.

XIII.
NOTE TO RODIN FROM RUE DE TURENNE, 1898

I've taken a new studio, in the Marais.
Never mind where, exactly.
This is just to tell you where I won't be.
Don't look for me. I want no
letters, no word from you at all,
unless it's to tell me Rose is dead,
and you poisoned her! Or that you're publishing
a confession, listing all your crimes
against me. Too late for anything else.
Everything you've said has turned to salt,
it penetrates the cracks in my skin,
so that I work all day with a sense
that my whole body's burning.
There's nothing more to say.

XIV.
QUAI BOURBON, 1900

My dear Paul,

This morning I woke with the taste of him
on my tongue. I spit and spit,
and the cats thought I was funny.
Too much work to do to think of him.
And the door is bolted. After my neighbor,
M. Picard, broke in with a passkey
and took back sketches of my *Yellow Woman,*
I learned to be careful.
Yellow women have appeared in two salons—
with Rodin's signature, of course!
Oh, he rakes it in—millions of francs
on my ideas. I wonder who's doing
his feet, who's carving eyes,
who poses for goodbyes and betrayals.
Rose was his model once, you know.
I saw her the time the cleaning woman
put drugs in my coffee, and I was out
for twelve whole hours. She was young,
swirling in bronze, then gold,
suspended from the ceiling—
then standing still, in stone.
Did you know she comes to my window
at night, peers in at me, sleeping?
I can hear her breath on the glass,
then a sound of choking.

xv.
DUST, 1907

Your bust is no more. It lived the life of roses.
                    —*Camille Claudel, in a letter to Henry Asselin*

My dear Paul,

July again, and nothing survives.
I begin to like my ritual:
all year I work as if the salons
were knocking on my door each week,
as if M. Dupin were waiting
for his commissions. I go out
into the streets to draw the people—
I want, now, my statues so distinct
from robber Rodin's that never
will anyone ask questions.
I choose a woman sweeping her doorstep,
her hair brushed back from her head,
not quite carelessly; a fat butcher
in his shop, a cleaver raised
in his hand; men building a fountain
in the square. Last week I saw two
on a scaffold, their brown arms lifting
sparkling pink granite. One's body was bent
powerfully in two by the weight,
and I'd already got them both in clay.
They're gone too. Everything.
I take the hammer and smash
whatever's there—clay, plaster,
marble, stone. It flies into the air
and becomes a million brilliant stars.
For hours, as the dark comes in, they go on
shining. I like to wander
through the debris, before the carter
comes to bury it. Now is the third
anniversary of my new life.

LETTER TO HER COUSIN CHARLES THIERRY

My dear Charles,

It's true—they locked me up! The very day
your letter came to tell me about Papa's death.
They buried him and didn't say

a word to me. Just as in Paris, the breath
of Rodin has soured the air at Villeneuve.
He meets the family secretly. They're tethered

to him the way I was, especially that naïve
Louise, my sister, who won't confess
to anything. A hundred thousand francs he bleeds

the public for, while the cats and I eat less
all the time, with no commissions to feed us.
When those brutes came to take me away—Blessed

Mary!—I begged them to let me smash
a few last things. Old casts of *Perseus*, four
fine ones, stood against one wall. They laughed.

I tried to write you then, but a nurse tore
up my letters. Mother wants to ban
me from writing anyone, calls me a whore

and lets me freeze here at Montdevergues, land
of the dying crazies. They scream day and night.
And the food! Worst in first class—it comes from cans

dribbled with poison. That's why I'm right
to stay in third, though I cook for myself
in any case—potatoes and eggs. It frightens

me how grateful I am to fill my poor shelf
once in a while with things from home—coffee,
sugar, soap, brandied cherries, half-melted

butter. Mother is kind about food, awfully
concerned for my health. But she never comes, never
answers my questions. Everyone says I'm softer

now, even docile. I'm sure I'd get better
at Villeneuve. I'd keep to myself—no sculpture—
nothing to make Mother angry. I could sit forever

in that garden, even forget the machinations of the monster
and his hag. I want the valley, those dark hills, my brother.

XVII.
DREAMS, 1920

My dear Paul,

This morning I woke to the sound
of a human voice in the chimney.
I knew who it was, for the night
had been filled with him. Months now,
I've had separate lives, the nightmare
day with its shrieking faces in every corner,
its greasy inedible soup, and the long
hours of my own silence, when the clouds
that used to hover over Villeneuve
descend around my head, so I
can scarcely see beyond the length
of my arm. Then the monster assumes
his proper form, and I'm on my guard.
But the nights! I'm taken back years,
to a bed in Touraine, to the bed
in La Folie Neubourg, to the studio
on Rue de l'Université. He takes me
in his arms. I'm twenty, nearly fainting
with desire. He's a volcano—unstoppable—
and I love his power, those enormous
insistent hands. Beautiful lies!

Sometimes I sculpt *Sea Foam* again—
that glistening marble torso
me, stretched on a tongue of onyx.
I strike a pose, he strides in,
strokes my hair and the curve of my back,
and I peer into his eyes.
I find them innocent! You must
be right. My mind turns itself
upside down.

Last things shall be
first, first last, love and hate
will clasp hands, whirl in a circle,
let go, and fall to the ground.

FROM THE ASYLUM AT MONTDEVERGUES, 1938

My dear Paul,

I wait for the visit you promised me
next summer, but I don't hope for it.
Paris is so far away, and God knows
what may happen.

At this holiday time I always dream
about Mother. I never saw her again
after the day you sent me to asylums.
I'm thinking of the portrait I did
of her in our garden—those large eyes
with their secret sadness, resignation
over her whole face, hands crossed
on her knees in total abnegation.
I never saw the portrait again either.
Surely that odious creature
I try not to name wouldn't have stolen
that too? Not a portrait of my mother!

From time to time they pretend
to improve my lot here, but it doesn't last.
It's a sham. Lately they built
a big kitchen, one kilometer away.
That gave me an outing and a walk.
Now I'm ordered not to go there anymore—
no reason. Oh how I long
to be in a real house, to be able
to shut the door properly.

My dear Paul, you poor sweet man—
they set you up in their game
without your even noticing.
The doctors said I could go home
years ago. Mother wouldn't have me
at Villeneuve. But you? You tell me
God has mercy on the afflicted,
God is good, etc. Let's talk about God,
who lets an innocent woman rot.

MANNA, SEPTEMBER, 1943

So much I finally understand—
how the spirit is nourished
by raisins and milk, how the days
disappear when you stay in bed,
so that one kind face bent
over your own is much
like another. Cakes arrive
in the mail from Paul.
I say to God, my cup
runneth over. I know
what it means. They tell me
I'm thin as a pine, but I eat
those gifts of jelly and butter,
I let sugar cubes melt on my tongue.
I remember pleasure,
my hands wet in plaster. I watch
a parade pass by my window, a line
of statues in bronze and marble,
bodies contorted, rising
and smiling, their lives
nearly over. Now they're erect,
growing younger
and younger, everything backward,
everything white.

Part Two

THIS BEGINNING

It is not a matter of adding more hatred to the world and of choosing between two societies, even though we know that American society represents the lesser evil. We don't have to choose evil, even the lesser.
—Manifesto of Groupes de Liaison Internationale, 1949

1942. *Combat* works to sabotage
German plans, to round up guns.
I'm born on a February morning.
It's cold. My mother is exhausted
by fear as well as the pain.
She's sleeping now, after
an agonized night
when dreams, in the intervals,
early, were of bombs
that fell on our house,
my bassinet shattered
and the fireplace rubble.
But we are in Rice Lake,
Wisconsin, as far from the war
as the woman who hides
Emmanuel and Henri Weiss,
ages ten and eleven,
in her Bordeaux attic
is from us.

I wake to the cries
of a dozen babies.
A nurse carries me in
to my mother,
bows tied in my
long black hair,
and she weeps.

Maria Casarès is playing
Deirdre of the Sorrows
in Paris. She meets Camus
for the first time, backstage.
Maria, who volunteered
in the Spanish Civil War
to work in hospitals,

who fainted when blood
spattered her dress, and again
at an amputation,
but who came back, day after day.
There are snapshots of me
in the arms of my uniformed father,
whose war was in the Pacific.
I'm wrapped in a blanket, eyes wide,
as my aproned grandmother
grins beside me.
Later I'll read his letters
to Mother,
of the mortar fire in his sleep,
the bravado of "when I get back."

Jean Bloch-Michel is arrested
and tortured.
Camus moves to 1-bis, Rue Vaneau,
to the studio apartment
adjoining Gide's. He's in hiding
here, where a trapeze hangs
from the ceiling.

I'm three, picking cotton, as a lark,
in a field near Fort Bragg,
bringing milk bottles in
from Mrs. Black's porch.

(Later, after the war,
our bodies fighter planes,
we children spread the wings
of our arms to dive the front yard,
yelling *Bombs Over Tokyo!*
We make the sounds of explosions,
spitting *Japs*
into the bat-filled dusk.
I have dreams of the mild
German grocer
who lives on my street.
He's a spy. I'm so sure
I implore my parents
to call the authorities.

While his thin and ascetic
pianist brother plays Chopin
across the street, I listen
beneath the window
for signs that he too
requires more attention.
Their sister comes out
on the porch, calling
"Who's there? Who are you children?"
The brother plays on, seeming
oblivious.

When Jacqueline Bernard
is arrested, the Gallimards
rush to Rue Vaneau
to remove Camus' clothes.
The next day three Gallimards
and the frail Camus
flee Paris on bicycles,
bound for a village,
a few days of relative safety.

They pedal back to the city
amid shells that land
in the fields at their sides,
convinced, this time,
"they are not meant for us."

Forty years later
a new acquaintance offers me
her small apartment,
1-bis, Rue Vaneau,
sans trapeze.
The tapestry hung on a wall
next to the courtyard window
depicts a France centuries ago.
No wars disturb its fragile fabric.
Two mathematicians
and Barbara and I drink wine
in that high-ceilinged room
until 3:00 A.M.
I sleep in the loggia, wake

too late to make a promised call
to a black friend
who, by the time I dress
and find a phone, has returned
to Germany. Germany,
where he feels freer, he says,
than in the U.S.

Now in Paris there are bombs
nearly every day.
While we listen to Ted Joans
read poems upstairs
at Shakespeare and Co.,
the Hotel de Ville post office
explodes. There's one in the lobby
of Barbara's hotel.
Beth is in front of TATI
minutes before the most recent
and worst: mothers with children
shopping to prepare for the *rentrée,*
the start of school.

Some define this as a war,
though, by comparison,
as Chirac says,
"It's only firecrackers,"
just a reminder
of what still burns in the dark.

Back home, a political poet
is being denied entrance
back into her country. Our
country. My mother is dreaming
again of bombs.

THERE ARE REASONS

to imagine mountains rising
out of the dark, as the real ones
reveal themselves at dawn,
pink clouds giving way
to violet, blue.
In the imaginary mountains
a man who has tended sheep all day
is crossing a stream so cold
his ankles ache, but he stops
and stands in the current,
listening to birds call,
to the rustle of leaves
that might mean someone is coming,
a woman shining like light
through the sprinkled leaves.
But she has arrived from the real
mountain, and does not see him there,
sees stone and fern and mushrooms
ripe for gathering. She does not hear
a hawk's wings as it lands yards away
in a tree. She will fill her basket
in silence, while the man watches
from a distance, holding his breath,
the song inside him contained
by his skin, by the walls
of his heart, softly beating.

NOW IS THE SILENCE OF SLEEPING DOVES

Of the neighbor's cough
quieted by codeine.
The silence of lovers
who've already forgotten
how the moon came to whiten
their open bodies. Now the hour
when breath wakens the skin
with its pauses.
From out of that stillness
a dog barks, then howls
as if the whole night
had been waiting,
as if, the dark being cleft
by that sound, all the wedges
could fall, deeper and deeper.

PORTRAIT

All those who do not know me think it an excellent likeness.

—André Gide

Behind the clear eyes, the panorama
of dream—that vast sea
with its lighthouse
of midnight, the glow easily mistaken
for the moon, waning in fog.
Someone shivers in a rowboat
drifting out of sight.

Who keeps the watch?
Someone is climbing the stairs
with a lantern.
He settles into a leather armchair
with the second volume
of a long biography, is lighting
a cigarette. He glances out
the tower's rounded windows
from time to time,
where a halo of misty light
keeps the distance from him.

Music is playing. Haydn.
Everything's in order.

Under the other moon
a figure is singing
or crying.
No one hears
as the boat rocks
on the small waves
getting larger.

THE MAN WHO LOVES COAL

Summer, a hint of fall,
then Indian summer—
my neighbor shovels coal.
His shed in the little courtyard
is filled to its long tin roof.
What can need to be done
in August, September, October,
when cold has not even put its foot
in the door? By 5:00 A.M. he's out there
shoveling, pouring coal through a chute.

Even the pigeons don't begin cooing
so early. By 7:00 I hear their wings.
But my neighbor gets up long before dawn
to his noisy, unaccountable work.

The woman who owns my apartment
complained to the city last year:
coal dust edges her new beige carpet
the length of the window wall.
The authorities promised action—
he's breaking a code.

Still, day after day I'm wakened
by the man whose mission it is
to worry coal.
His ground-floor apartment
is tiny as mine;
what does it take to warm him?
Does he dream of winters
in Sweden, long enough to need fire
until May, and night enough to absorb him?

What draws a man out of his bed
to break the summery silence
scraping   scraping
a concrete floor,
revising places for coal?

THAT JOURNEY

London, and the light is falling.
Lost, trying to follow any

street to the river,
I come upon fork after fork.

Always I take the left.
When the bank

of the Thames comes almost clear,
I'm miles from a phone.

Even the fog is darker
than reason, a few shop lights

show faces I'd rather not meet.
Running on a highway

outside the city, I spot a taxi,
wave him down. It's you

I'm thinking of. So late,
and no word. Passing a restaurant,

I read a sign, a menu:
International Cuisine becomes

Irrational Desire. Streetlights
dim in the rising dawn,

a naked man pounds on a door,
his clothes strewn

through the garden. A woman
rises out of her coma

to greet me. She is an angel.
Beautiful, her face is swollen

on one side only. She holds out
her hand, and I take it.

GENÊT

for Daryl

This is for you, who loved him, though
you never met, except through words
like high notes making a long glissando
down the page.

I've just learned that my favorite
French wildflowers, ones
with long bright stems and heavy clusters
of yellow blossoms, bear his name.
Yesterday I gathered them in heaps, the way
I did last summer, remembering
how one big brandy snifter lets them
fill half a room.

You'll like it that they have to be cut
with a knife, they're that tough,
and that it's hard to wedge the stems
between rocks set in the glass base
to keep them from tipping over.

A year ago I walked through these same fields
and didn't know the names of anything.
Margueritas filled my smaller vases,
and I called them daisies.

My friend Edmund spends his time
writing Genêt's biography. Another
act of love this chilly summer,
when no one knows how long
the season can last.

All year I have been redefining love.
You know about that. I wish you could know
the fragrance that fills this house.
I wish I could give you time
in these mountains, and brilliant genêts.

AFTER THIRTY OCTOBERS

This weather brings back Sunday
after church, reading the St. Paul paper,
the fragrance of lemon pie drifting
into the living room. Gary's stretched
on the floor with the funnies. David's pulling
boxing gloves off and on, caressing
his own soft fists. Mary Jo brings me
grape juice in a glass so small I tease her—
it's Second Communion. Not yet a beauty,
her almond eyes are magnified
behind thick glasses. She's seven and I'm fifteen,
drowsy against the heat register we dispute over.
Dad's alive, coming in from the meadow
where he's been talking with horses. This afternoon
he'll make fence—the sorrel, Flame, following,
nuzzling his back. Dinner's ready,
Mother's heaping pork chops onto a platter.
The grapefruit tree in the corner has spread
its leaves to the steam wafting out from the kitchen,
is fuller and greener than it will be
again. When the phone rings it's the boy
I'll marry, who's on his way, innocent
as the Siamese cat who suddenly drags
used Kotex all over the house. I run room
to room, scooping up bloody pads. Sun streams
into the cage of the new canary, who's just
stopped singing. Through the window we watch
tall field grass ripple and change, bend deep
and white in wind. I go out to stand in it,
as under the darkening sky, it's become ocean.

NEW PHYSICS

And if we should collide with such force,
might we fly off in different directions
and disappear, leaving, in our place,
some new combination that isn't us, really?
I've always imagined your fear
was something like that, even before
there was a language to explain it. Now
I think I partly understand
your flight, after love, from the room
where we watched through open windows
the stars and their discrete pulsing.

I speak of this, of you, as if we were
still present tense, as if you hadn't
once more approached the rim of my life,
that wobbly circumference, then chosen,
again, a safe trajectory. Once a month,
on schedule, I retrace those paths
as if there were something new I could learn,
some variable I might change,
and the world would be different.

Even these thousands of miles
do not annihilate your pull.
When you are asleep and dreaming,
I turn toward the visible moon, pale
in a daytime sky, and feel myself spinning.

SAFE COMPANIONS

1.

Such recognitions as the heart
finds in the tribute
you come across unexpectedly
in a journal, and equally
in a Russian voice lifting
poem after poem above despair,
become the easier access
to what you hope to discover.
Nobody in the bed
still trying to sleep
as you drop a log
on the pine floor,
as you clatter around
in the kitchen.
No large or small betrayal
waiting to be enacted. Here,
letting its guard down,
the body forgets itself
in the ordinary rituals
of each slow day. In words
patient as the house
whose language you are learning.

2.

Remember when you thought
a little time could buy wisdom?
That solitude alone
and the absence of work
could take you
through your whole childhood
and back, the ancient cutter
sliding over snow as on the family's
snapshot Christmas cards,
the black mare your father cursed
in the only Norwegian
you ever learned
rearing, protesting her role,
but taking you, nonetheless.
And at the end of that long ride

on the frozen back roads
you'd climb down, and all
your letters home after that
would be different,
and you'd find every day simpler.

3.

When your watch quits
and you're in the middle of somewhere
other people would call nowhere,
all alone, and the days stretch
from light to darkness
without conversation
other than the radio's, you begin
to talk to yourself, almost
normally, to speculate
on what it means if the sun
has begun to set before
you've had lunch.
It's like living with an aunt
who pays attention
to your smallest actions—
how carefully you wash the dishes
and whether the edges of the toast
are *too* burned, or just the way
she secretly likes them.
Sometimes she frets, wonders
if the bowl of fruit on the table
will last until the next time
someone comes with a car.
On a rainy day
there are fewer guidelines,
pine trees drifting into view
and disappearing
as if night were coming on,
and then an unexpected brightening.
Though you have many books,
you go to bed with an old magazine,
glad for a familiar voice
rising from the page,

taking you to another place
when you were someone else
and younger.

4.

No matter how many autumn mountains
you gaze at, how many
clouds you watch pushing
each other through the sky,
there come those moments
in the solitary day
when a mother's quiet weeping
will startle you. Whose voice?
The child, waking to strange light,
when snow has completely
covered the north windows,
speaks too, with an understanding
you don't remember, an apprehension
accurate and vague.
How far you will go to escape!
Into the playhouse
with its handmade blue furniture.
Into the fields you rode through
on horseback, where daisies
grew tall enough
that a boy you loved could gallop
through, full speed, bending down
to pluck them for you.
Into another country
whose landscape fades in
and out perpetually.

PARIS AUBADE

Breathing, the last possession
that counts, comes faster here, where
time and our oldest obsessions

make us more conscious—self-conscious. The air
is completely polluted, of course, but haze
that descends on this city is like the fair

skin of Doris Day, filmed in the days
when soft light meant dropping gauze
in front of the camera. It's like that these lazy

first weeks when we stay in bed until noon, lawless
as coupling cats we hear on the balcony, late.
We inhale each morning as if the flawed

fabric of earlier lives had been laid
in a drawer, carefully folded, forever.
Yet under the net of that dream, we pay

for what we know. Bodies that flail under covers
all hours in pleasure learn to count breaths—
just after. Though the world falls away for lovers

as they make the escape into flesh,
its heavy atmosphere fills them. Clouds
are the color of nipples. Worn silk thins to mesh.

LIVING IN THE COUNTRY, JUST BEFORE MARRIAGE

We'd been here weeks when the snake
appeared on the stairs, slithered
over a foot on its way between
bedrooms. Probably, we said,
they've been here all the time,
their lives spent under the steps,
in the walls behind chipped plaster.
We thought we saw the tip of a tail
sticking out. Scott prodded the hole
with a knife, but it was gone.

We walk calmly up and down
as if this were a metaphor, the glimmering
scales invented in that twilight hour
when dreams turn language around
and around, so that it coils
on itself, its raised head swaying
to its own sibilant music, measuring
pleasure in the rhythms of its tongue.

LAURA

And now we are three—one of us
still swathed in the scarves
of childhood, peeling them off, one
after another, pastel cotton plaids
giving way to silk in a range
of tulip colors. She emerges
with her dark hair tangled,
the way she likes it.

And what if this is not just
the beginning, what if this is
the moment we pass without noticing,
when the senses tell us everything
we'll know? She can sniff a star-white
flower on the side of the road
and say when it released its pollen,
when its embroidered blossoms
will become dust.

She consumes the planets with her
perfect vision, with a red telescope
set on the balcony table. All night
we hear her above us, shifting
position, taking notes on the universe.

A STORY FOR OUR TIME

I.

A Cathar woman believed the devil
could come in the night,
trailing a herd of sheep, the dogs
yipping at their heels, vague
familiar warnings. He might
assume the guise of an ordinary man,
who'd ask her, friendly as a brother,
to peel the rawhide from his skin,
to pluck the lice from his body.
All night, like a kind neighbor,
she'd draw his individual hairs
between her nails, rub oil
into his scalp by candlelight,
until the dawn when, dizzied
by cold, they fell into her straw bed.
Sometimes he'd be a priest, a *parfait*,
who'd abjured the flesh of woman
forever, but found December's
holy story inverting his dreams,
and like a man sleepwalking,
slid into her house, onto her pallet,
the serpent in him. They saw
the power, the light transfigured
when God was asleep, so that
his enemy gained the upper hand.
Afterward they were ashamed,
fasted and prayed, for the devil
had force like the wind from Africa,
blowing sand in their eyes.
They chose how to die—no water
or food until purity evaporated flesh.

But the true church found other ways.
Heretic tenets of poverty struck
to the hearts of pockets, made popes
lift furious fists, cardinals caress
their gold medallions with the fervor
of anxious lovers. And to say
the devil had magic equal to His!

47

Whole villages marched to the fires.
At the foot of our chateau,
they perished like Jews.
Hard to root out from these hills,
but a few at a time, their spirits
flew from the flames
to be reborn, again and again,
to Satan's earth.

2.

Jesus lusts for a woman.
He fantasizes thighs, skin silver
as coins in the temple, but warm,
soft, himself disappearing
into her blue robes like diving
into clear Adriatic waters, deep,
under a high noon sky.
In Paris, the Cinema St. Michel,
showing *The Last Temptation
of Christ,* is burned to the ground.
Its gutted interior smoulders
for days. True believers throng
the theaters all over France,
waving their placards like swords,
torches piled in the trunks of cars.
When someone gives the word,
the righteous threaten to rise
once again, to melt His filthy
flesh from the screen of every town,
no matter how remote, erasing
that blasphemous body
from the sacred earth.

DREAMING THE LATEST VERSION

The signs are in the sky
and the radio tells us:
those dark pink clouds that rest
like clots on the darker horizon
contain the seeds of our death,
and we are ready.

All the major powers have agreed—
one final, surprising accord—
to hasten the end. As the clouds
come down, planes will fly over,
dropping a quick gas,
making it painless.

My brother calls to ask if I have
new thoughts on the afterlife.
I am amazed, I say,
to observe that I am not even curious.
Nor am I, who have always feared death,
afraid. Most of us are calm.

Mother and I make a pact to hold hands.
My son, too young to understand,
changes his shoes.
Only one of our number becomes ambitious—
wishes to do what he has not done
in a lifetime. He paints. He starts a story.
But after a few frantic hours
he changes his mind and rests.

We wonder what will happen to books.
How long before pottery disappears.

I decide to forgive everyone
who's ever hurt me. I begin
listing them in my head
and say to myself
that if there should be
a last-minute reprieve

(impossible, but for a moment
or two, the thought occurs)
my word will stand:
I will not feel rancor again.

My sister and I stand at the window
remarking changes in the wind.

Part Three

AU PREMIER COUP

There are moments we record
so indelibly that when
the smell of popcorn, say, or
a phrase from Grieg wafts across
the room, you see a mother
standing at a bathinette,
a baby fat and slippery under her hands,
piles of cotton diapers on a shelf
in three neat stacks, white
as blossoms. It's a quarter
of a century ago, and more.
You're young as the cherry tree
outside the opalescent window.
In your dreams, you sit in its branches,
looking through the glass
at yourself, bathing the child.
Framed like that, you're held,
the picture's surface
opaque, no underpainting
showing through. Someone
shakes an aluminum pot
in the kitchen. The sounds
of popping corn are grace
notes falling through the evening air.

THESE WORLDS

I forget who said that art is to reality as wine is to grapes, but it's a brilliant remark.

—Vsevold Meyerhold

Fog descends with a vengeance, obscuring
the lines we used to guide ourselves
on one crooked path, past rosebushes set
at random among fields of weeds, and dirty
Holsteins, houses falling to ruin.
Geraniums and impatiens at those windows
are babies, leaning from playpens;
old women on hard chairs embroider and nod
before their heavy doors. We elevate
all this, wait for skies that justify
the world, the sun setting rose over
two humped peaks, the benevolent snake
of cloud that leaves a gap between
the ridge to the east and the vast
mixed and scuttling blue. Fragrant pink bells
grow close to the bridge, where we've mostly
learned to avoid the nettles that can sting
three days. Worth it anyway. On the dining-
room table, stained with fifty years
of wine bottles, hoops spiraling
like a chain of genes, and spilled
olive oil, they radiate sweetness, last
a few days, lanterns
against the dark. Now the sky
is a Rothko, its middle panel a subtler
gray than usual, while below
a pale strip promises transformation.

NOCTURNE

Translated into sheet music and performed on the piano, a portion of mouse RNA sounds like a lively waltz.

—*Susumu Ohno*

Last night we heard him
in the cupboard, that scrabbling
familiar noise jolting us
from our French lesson,
whose sounds are not so etched
in our brains. While the tape
played *Une hirondelle ne fait pas
le printemps*, I thought of the mice
born beneath my kitchen sink
one spring, their feet slipping
and scratching in the night.

It's not exactly fear
that makes me start—
but I sleep uneasily,
hearing Chopin,
the notes like steps I must take
up and down a staircase,
at first too quick for comfort.

The scene shifts—a field
opens before me, full
of white and purple daisies.
The ground remembers me—
aroma of sweet earth,
soft fragrant hay, just cut.
Somewhere in my bones
a harp plays, now a flute.

DREAMING THE SUMMER NIGHTS: SCANDINAVIAN PAINTINGS FROM THE TURN OF THE CENTURY

One must close the eyes at times, dream of what one has seen, transform it, and weigh the varied impressions the eyes have received against feeling in order to fathom the unity in this barbaric multifariousness.

—Richard Bergh

All old religious ideas are awakening and a time of new mysticism, new occult doctrines, invocations of the spirits and star gazing wafts through the intellectual life of the end of the century. The human spirit once again feels the need to fall on its knees before the great unknown spirit of the world.

—Eino Leino

1. *Wounded Angel*, Hugo Simberg, 1903

The angel rides between poles
two sturdy boys carry the way
they'd carry lumber, or push
a wheelbarrow. They are glum,
reluctant, perhaps, but accustomed
to heavy chores. The angel is tired,
and her head hurts. Her wings droop
in an arc, hair brushing her ankles,
while her hands, still clutching
daisies, grip the poles. It's a delicate
balance. Bruised under feathers,
it's hard to sit like that
for long. The muscles are already
sore. The boys know who she is,
but they're too young to be scared.
They follow the path by the lake,
the angel almost weeping now,
head bowed,
her blonde hair brushing
her cheeks like tears.
The bandage has slipped
down over her eyes,
her bare feet are cold.

2. By *Lamplight*, Harriet Backer, 1890

A puff of curtain at the stark window
the only softness in this room
where a woman lives. We feel
her absorption in a book,
how it takes her out of her body
seated on a hard chair
at a plain pine table.
She's wearing heavy wool.
The stove is lit, but there's little
warmth under gray rafters, within
these variegated walls. Outside,
the night hisses cold. Her concentration
seems undisturbed, and we like
to imagine she's entered a chamber,
not alone, where lamplight flickers
over plush sofas, and a fire
hot enough to warm a grand salon
makes her strong features gentle,
her bare arms gold. But what if
she has chosen the hard white light
of her present, where illumination
is confined to half the table,
her book and face? Here
is no romanticizing of the shadows,
here is where, every night, she goes.

3. *Riddarfjarden in Stockholm*, Eugene Jansson, 1898

The bay delivers itself of light,
sharp spears fading
into the background, as a luminous body
floats into view. At the horizon,
signs of an ordinary life, the day somewhere
in a distance, not yet distinguishable.
For the moment, everything drifts
in blackness, in bruise-blue,

under an enclosing sky. The moment
of full awakening is hours away,
buildings do not yet blink
nor acknowledge a streak of red,
a notice of what begins, and of what dies.

4. *After Sunset*, Kitty L. Kielland, 1886

Before a great wooden house lifted
on pillars above the sloping grass,
a lake shines in prolonged
dusk. Among clusters of green,
floating unanchored in the black,
a woman in a rowboat looks back
out over the lake to something
we can't see. She lifts her oars,
drifts into shadow.

A horse grazes in the yard,
almost as still as the water.
Dark has begun in the trees,
and the house is dark
under clouds still tinged
with pink—the sun's trail,
long as summer, as life.

5. *Symposium* (*The Problem*), Askeli Gallen-Kallela, 1894

Men stare at the bird's red wings, Osiris
appearing after dinner, after the brandy,
as if to the summons of a voice. Sibelius
holds its eyes with his own, he's slouched
relaxed, a cigarette dangling
from his fingers. Only
the painter himself is more disturbed
than entranced. Someone rests
his head on the table, having seen

too much. The Finnish night fills
with crimson clouds, while Jupiter burns
in place, and stars are scattered like grain
more visible than the full moon
should allow. A tree behind them,
blacker than sky, invites the bird.
They are young, the winds of the world
are swirling around them.

6. *The Sick Girl*, Ejnar Nielsen, 1896

*I do not understand why people cannot view death, with its majestic beauty,
as they can life.*

　　　　　　　　　　　　　　　　　　　—Ejnar Nielsen

The tent her knees make with the blanket
is a knobbed mountain
whose furrows run down in shadow.
She looks at that peak
where nothing grows—no pine,
no moss, and imagines herself
sliding from the summit, all the way
down to the valley of her body.
Her hand, gripping the rail
of the iron bed, is hollows
and bone, her fine thin face
could have been sculpted from marble.
In the narrow, cramped bed,
she's warm, near the stove,
and there contemplates its forged
details—garlands surrounding a baby.
She can't be more than sixteen.
Her concerns are defined
by the contours of sheets, a plaid
shawl folded under her head,
a vision of herself lifting
toward the rafters.

7. *Boys Bathing in the Sea on a Summer Evening*, Peder Severin Kroyer, 1899

The moon's shattered topaz skitters
down the water. Two naked boys,
whose skin in bright light
would be milk, here are
candescent. One runs in, chilled,
from shallow water,
the other rests on shore,
drying his feet. A girl waves
to a ship, is making her slow
way there. At the blue hour,
even the sand is burnished,
even the simple earth.

8. *The Storm*, Edvard Munch, 1893

Asgardstrand in summer.
The sky is heavy as a woman
before she bleeds.

Young women stand huddled
in the dark, their backs
to the lighted house
which shines harshly,
like a father waving a lantern,
calling their names,
calling them to come in,
it's late, to their cool beds.

They listen to nothing—not
the blaring light,
not thunder in the background.

The one in white moves
as if she's asleep
toward water.

9.   *The Voice, ca.* 1893, Edvard Munch

Between the couple in the boat
rowing toward the moon
pitched into the water
like desire, and the woman
standing, her face lifted
as for a kiss, but with hands
clasped behind her,
pines.
They divide the water
and the beach into discrete
strips, the way
the mind divides. Stones
are eyes. The red edge
of the sand runs thinly down.

10.   *Ashes,* Edvard Munch, 1896

She is bewildered by his
terror, his despair,
which rise again
like desire, its aftermath.
The smoking log
could be water,
the trunk of a live tree
melting into it.
She stretches, makes small
attempts to repair her hair
while he bends to his hands,
love gone,
his face gray as the shore.

11.   *Dance on the Shore,* Edvard Munch, 1900/1902

The beach is a mouth,
a whole face and a mouth
on which two young women
whirl, clasping each other's hands
and leaning back
into the almost-wind.

The aunts disapprove
or pretend to
but stay
where the moon slides
through trees, down
across rippling water.

Everyone knows the black
they must walk through,
home.

But Sigrid and Karla
pretend they don't,
and nobody sees the red.

TO ENTER

on a marble sculpture by Nicolae Fleissig

Believe that veined wings heavy as memory
might, any moment, fold from the spine
of sorrow and take off into night.
Now, under moonlight, they lean
toward a curve of back, rest against flesh.

Prepare for a book of water in wind, for pages
open to the sun, music on stands rippling
black under plane trees. Yes, here are the closed
petals of sex, there is a head
like the whole body of a jellyfish, translucent
inside its pale helmet.

Think of a man with wooden blinders, each
painted with ancient worlds, so that when
they are shut, he contemplates golden dragons,
bracelets with rubies circling
bone-white arms. When the panels are open,
the light coming in is pain.

Though teeth grin the body's defiance,
the body's knowledge, mountains are rising
from plains.

There are paths to lost cities, to the heart's
magnificent ruins.